T0166066

Bible, Prayer, and Miracles

Paddleduck #5

AUNT JULIE

Order this book online at www.trafford.com
or email orders@trafford.com

Most Trafford titles are also available at major online book retailers.

© Copyright 2011 Aunt Julie.
All rights reserved. No part of this publication may be reproduced, stored in a retrieval
system, or transmitted, in any form or by any means, electronic, mechanical, photocopying,
recording, or otherwise, without the written prior permission of the author.

Printed in the United States of America.

ISBN: 978-1-4669-0012-7 (sc)
ISBN: 978-1-4669-0033-2 (e)

Trafford rev. 12/06/2011

 www.trafford.com

North America & international
toll-free: 1 888 232 4444 (USA & Canada)
phone: 250 383 6864 ♦ fax: 812 355 4082

I want to thank all my friends for their contributions, Irene Cassis, Victoria Sarvadi, Cheryl Watkins, and all of the children from St. Mary's. I really appreciate your help. Thank you all,

Julie Pierce

Dear Friends and Family,

The bible is not just a book. It is our guidelines for living. We are all sinners. It is a sin to pass judgment on others. It is a sin not to forgive others. Be honest with yourself. You have to put one foot in front of the other one day at a time. I heard a sermon once and the pastor said, "Jesus is not enough until he is all there is". I have had times when I felt lonely, afraid, or maybe I needed help with a decision. God is always there for us and listening. Don't wait for something to happen to turn to Jesus. Be prepared for anything that happens and pray every day. Read your bible.

Aunt Julie

MIRACLES AND PRAYER.

I strongly believe in the power of prayer and I know miracles do happen. In 1993 my sister Carolyn had a severe asthma attack and one lung collapsed. Her heart stopped briefly and she saw the white light you hear people talk about with near death experiences. The oxygen was cut off to the brain and the doctors told us to prepare for the worst. She was in a coma for 10 days. We didn't know how she would be when she woke up. My friend Debbie brought some Holy Water from Yugoslavia where the virgin mother Mary had been seen in a vision. The movie, Song of Bernadette, was made about it. We would not accept defeat. When Carolyn awoke she knew everyone in the room. She did have some memory loss but the doctors said it was a miracle. They expected her to be brain dead. She is well now but her pulmonary system is still very fragile and she has to take special care of her health. In 2000, my sister Kathy had breast cancer. The doctors gave her 50/50 chance if she had a double mastectomy and half her limp nodes removed. She went through Chemo and Radiation. Again, dad prayed to God for the same angels that took care of Carolyn to take care of Kathy. We went with Kathy to a nutritionist for cancer patients, Caroline Sutherland. We all went on the cancer diet to build and boost the immune system. Praise God, he wasn't ready for her. Eleven years later, God did answer our prayers and Kathy is a cancer survivor.

Mat 4:23   And Jesus went about all Galilee, teaching in their synagogues, and preaching the gospel of the kingdom, and healing all manner of sickness and all manner of disease among the people.

At a time when the world is in such political and economical uncertainty we can find great comfort in the message that Jesus taught as He explained the gospel of the kingdom. The message of the kingdom, although different than the gospel of salvation (which is the Good News that we can be saved from our sinful state through the blood of the Lamb of God which was shed on our behalf), is none the less just as powerful! The Gospel or message of the kingdom is this: Yeshua (Hebrew for Jesus), the lamb, is also the Lion coming back to set up His Kingdom here on planet Earth! The Lord is coming back to conquer all that is evil and bring genuine peace to our world. He has authority (even now) over every sickness and disease and even death. He will rule all nations in fairness and with justice.

We, who love the Lord, can all look forward to world of peace and victory one day. May all who read the pages of this book find blessing and encouragement on every page!

Victoria Sarvadi, THD

From the beginning, the early church has had a tradition of using Worship, Personal Prayer and living the sacramental life of the church to help us grow in Christ. Worship began in the Jewish temple, and Christianity continued this tradition in the church in the form of liturgy. Liturgy simply means "work of the people". It is important for all of us to come together as the church and pray for one another and the world in which we live. Personal prayer is as important as participating in liturgy. It is another more personal way of talking to God and seeking His guidance.

The sacraments are God's way of showing us how to live our life as Christians. We come into the church through the sacrament of Baptism. This is the beginning of our spiritual life in Christ. Receiving Holy Communion is yet another way of being nourished by Him to continue this journey.

Living in Christ so that we can become Christ-like is the goal of all Christians. Worship, personal prayer and partaking of the sacramental life of the church are the examples Christ has given us in His Word. Let us be attentive to what He has to say in the Bible.

Irene Cassis, Director of Religious Education
Annunciation Greek Orthodox Cathedral

The Lord's Prayer

Our Father, which art in heaven,
hallowed be thy name.
Thy Kingdom come,
thy will be done,
in earth as it is in heaven
Give us this day our daily bread.
And forgive us our trespasses,
as we forgive those that trespass against us.
And lead us not into temptation,
but deliver us from evil.
For thine is the kingdom,
The power, and the glory,
Forever and ever.
Amen.

Matthew 6: 9-13

The Miracles of Jesus in the Gospels of Matthew, Mark, Luke, John

Word Scramble

Clramlei _____

Ratwe _____

Isdclepi _____

Teksab _____

Nbidl _____

Mrsto _____

Hsfi _____

Rdeba _____

Nghleai _____

sseuJ _____

RAISING OF LAZARUS

Lazarus was a boy who was very sick. Mary and Martha said Jesus, "Come quick!" Jesus did not come when Mary asked Him to. Jesus had a plan; he knew what He would do. Lazarus had died. When Jesus got to him, Jesus cried because Lazarus was His friend. Jesus hurt when he saw that everyone was sad but Jesus knew how quick people would be glad. Jesus came to the rock where Lazarus lay. Jesus told the people to push the rock away. When the rock was gone, Jesus began to shout. People heard Him say, "Lazarus, come out!" Jesus made Lazarus come back to life again people believed in Jesus because He helped their friend.

THE GREAT CATCH

Jesus and his disciples were out on the lake when a storm suddenly
came up. Jesus was asleep in the boat and his friends were afraid.
They woke him. He got up and told the storm to stop and it was
completely calm. The wind stopped blowing and the water was still.
His disciples were amazed. "Even the winds and the waves obey him,"
they said.

And he arose, and rebuked the wind and said unto the sea, "Peace, be
still." And the wind ceased, and there was a great calm.

Mark 4:39

WATER INTO WINE

Jesus went to a wedding and the wine was all gone His mother, Mary, came to Him to tell Him what was wrong. Jesus answered Mary, "My time has not yet come," Mary did not understand but listened to her Son. She told the servants to obey what Jesus told them to do they filled six jugs with water And Jesus made wine new.

JESUS WALKS ON WATER

Jesus fed the people, and then went off to pray; His friends got in the boat and went far away. Jesus' friends, the disciples, did not know what to think. The sea's waves were very high they thought their boat would sink. But Jesus came to them by walking on the sea. The disciples were afraid until Jesus said, "It's me." Jesus told Peter he could walk on water too Peter climbed out of the boat and knew just what to do. But as he walked across the sea Peter saw the great big waves He thought that he might sink and he became afraid. He called out to Jesus and was saved right away but Jesus then told Peter "You have little faith." The disciples had been watching and there was not even one who did not now believe That Jesus as God's Son.

JESUS FEEDS FIVE THOUSAND

The little boy offered to Jesus all he had five loaves and two fishes made the people glad For Jesus took this small amount and made it multiply He blessed the loaves and fishes while looking to the sky.

JESUS HEALS

Jesus healed Simon Peter's mother-in-law who had a dangerous fever. She got up and served them. Matthew 8:14-15

He healed the nobleman's son without going to the child. John 4:46-54

He once cleansed a leper, but warned him to say nothing. However, the man spread the news all around. Mark 1:40-45

There was a man in Jerusalem who had been blind from birth. Jesus put clay on the blind man's eyes and told him to go wash in the pool of Siloam. When he washed the clay off, he could see. John 9:1-41

Once in Jerusalem, a blind beggar named Bartimaeus asked Jesus for mercy and healing. Jesus told him that his faith had cured him and the man praised God for his sight. Mark 10:46-52

Word Scramble Answers—Miracle, water, disciple, basket, blind, storm, fish, bread, healing, Jesus

Miracles of Jesus

S	O	L	X	T	S	A	E	F	B	D	W
U	E	V	E	A	M	L	S	E	L	E	A
S	N	L	H	P	C	R	G	H	W	B	S
E	Y	I	P	A	R	G	O	N	M	L	H
J	Q	W	R	I	A	O	H	T	F	U	A
M	P	I	N	R	C	G	S	I	S	F	M
L	M	W	I	N	E	S	G	Y	D	K	A
K	A	H	W	E	D	D	I	N	G	N	Z
F	L	K	F	O	O	R	I	D	P	A	E
B	N	A	E	L	G	L	S	O	O	H	D
M	Q	Y	W	R	B	R	O	P	V	T	E
F	E	P	K	Z	R	L	C	I	G	Z	A

AMAZED	BED	BEGGAR
BLIND	DISCIPLES	FEAST
JESUS	LAKE	LEPROSY
MIRACLE	POOL	ROOF
STORM	THANKFUL	WALK
WASH	WEDDING	WINE

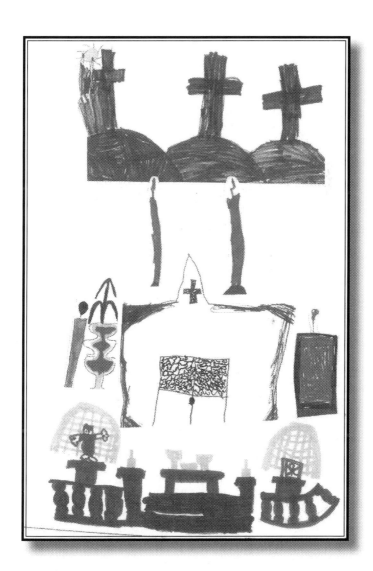

FAVORITE BIBLE VERSES

For God so loved the world that he gave his one and only Son, that
whoever believes in him shall not perish but have eternal life.
John 3:16

For all have sinned and fall short of the glory of God.
Romans 3:23

I will teach you wisdom's ways and lead you in straight paths.
Proverbs 4:11

Jesus replied:" 'Love the Lord your God with all your heart and with
all your soul and with all your mind.' This is the first and greatest
commandment. And the second is like it: 'Love your neighbor
as yourself."
Matthew 22:37-39

Do not judge others, and you will not be judged.
Matthew 7:1

Do not be anxious about anything, but in everything, by prayer and petition, with thanksgiving, present your requests to God.
Philippians 4:6

Do not let your hearts be troubled. Trust in God; trust also in me."
John 14:1

For where two or three gather together as my followers, I am there among them." Then Peter came to him and asked, "Lord, how often should I forgive someone who sins against me? Seven times?" "No, not seven times," Jesus replied, "but seventy times seven!
Matthew 18:20-22

The Nicene Creed is the creed or profession of faith (Greek: Σύμβολον τῆς Πίστεως) that is most widely used in Christian liturgy. It is called Nicene because, in its original form, it was adopted in the city of Nicaea by the first ecumenical council, which met there in the year 325.

Nicene Creed

I believe in one God, Father Almighty, Creator of heaven and earth, and of all things visible and invisible. And in one Lord Jesus Christ, the only-begotten Son of God, begotten of the Father before all ages; Light of Light, true God of true God, begotten, not created, of one essence with the Father through whom all things were made. Who for us men and for our salvation came down from heaven and was incarnate of the Holy Spirit and the Virgin Mary and became man. He was crucified for us under Pontius Pilate, and suffered and was buried; And He rose on the third day, according to the Scriptures. He ascended into heaven and is seated at the right hand of the Father; And He will come again with glory to judge the living and dead. His kingdom shall have no end. And in the Holy Spirit, the Lord, the Creator of life, Who proceeds from the Father, Who together with the Father and the Son is worshipped and glorified, Who spoke through the prophets. In one, holy, catholic, and apostolic Church. I confess one baptism for the forgiveness of sins. I look for the resurrection of the dead, and the life of the age to come.

Amen.

Apostles Creed

I believe in God the Father Almighty, Maker of heaven and earth.
And in Jesus Christ his only Son our Lord; who was conceived by the
Holy Ghost, born of the Virgin Mary, suffered under Pontius Pilate,
was crucified, dead, and buried; he <u>descended</u> into hell; the third day
he rose again from the dead; he ascended into heaven, and sitteth
on the right hand of God the Father Almighty; from thence he shall
come to judge the quick and the dead.

I believe in the Holy Ghost; the holy Catholic Church; the
communion of saints; the forgiveness of sins; the resurrection of the
body; and the life everlasting.

Amen.

Ava Maria

Hail Mary, full of grace, the Lord is with Thee.
Blessed art Thou among women
And Blessed is the fruit of Thy womb, Jesus.

Holy Mary, Mother of God
Pray for us sinners now and at the hour of our death.
Amen

I PLEDGE ALLEGIANCE

TO THE

FLAG,

OF THE UNITED

STATES OF AMERICA,

AND TO THE REPUBLIC, FOR

WHICH IT STANDS,

<u>ONE</u>

<u>NATION UNDER GOD,</u>

INDIVISIBLE,

WITH LIBERTY

AND JUSTICE FOR ALL!

BOOKS OF THE BIBLE

Old Testament

The Law: Genesis, Exodus, Leviticus, Numbers, Deuteronomy

History: Joshua, Judges, Ruth, 1 Samuel, 2 Samuel, 1 Kings, 2 Kings, 1 Chronicles, 2 Chronicles, Ezra, Nehemiah, Esther

Poetry & Wisdom: Job, Psalms, Proverbs, Ecclesiastes, Song of Solomon

Major Prophets: Isaiah, Jeremiah, Lamentations, Ezekiel, Daniel

Minor Prophets: Hosea, Joel, Amos, Obadiah, Jonah, Micah, Nahun, Habakkuk, Zephaniah, Haggai, Zechariah, Malachi

New Testament

The 4 Gospels: Matthew, Mark, Luke, John

Acts: Acts

Paul's Letters: Romans, 1 Corinthians, 2 Corinthians, Galatians, Ephesians, Philippians, Colossians, 1 Thessalonians, 2 Thessalonians, 1 Timothy, 2 Timothy, Titus, Philemon

General Epistles: Hebrews, James, 1 Peter, 2 Peter, 1 John, 2 John, 3 John, Jude, Revelation

IMPORTANT BOOKS OF THE BIBLE

Genesis

This is the first book of the Bible which comes in the Old Testament. It mainly focuses on the creation of the world, Adam and Eve, and how sin entered mankind. It also includes stories of Noah's Ark, Abraham and Isaac, Esau and Jacob, Joseph, and other histories. The book of Genesis gives information about major things that happened in the world. Many of the <u>Bible fun facts</u> are recorded in the book of Genesis.

Psalms

Psalms is the 19th book in the Old Testament, which includes around 150 songs and prayers that are sorted out according to chapters and <u>Bible verses</u>. A majority of these songs were written by King David. In this book, you will come across several <u>prayers</u> appropriate to be made to God. Most of the verses are also used in a large number of songs sung by Christian singers and musicians today.

Proverbs

This book of the Bible has wise sayings, <u>inspirational quotes</u>, and rules for living. It is believed that this book was written by Solomon who was King David's son. For Bible readers who have just started out, it is suggested that you read one chapter a day. Meditating on the verses in the book of Proverbs will surely make you wise enough to deal with any kind of situation that you come across.

The Gospels

The Gospels refer to four of the first books in the New Testament which depict the birth, growth, purpose, death, and the resurrection of <u>Jesus Christ</u>. There are four gospels namely; Gospel of Matthew, Gospel of Mark, Gospel of Luke, and Gospel of John in the Christian Bible. The 'Gospel of Matthew' was written by Matthew who was Jesus' disciple, whereas the 'Gospel of Mark' by Mark, and so on. All the Gospels are based on the same concept but presented in a different manner with some additional elements from the life of Jesus Christ.

Revelation

For many Bible scholars, this is the most interesting book in the Bible. The book of Revelation concentrates on the future and end of the world which is to come. It mentions the signs of the last times, coming of the Messiah, the rapture, judgment day, the war between <u>God</u> and Satan, and a formation of a totally new earth and heaven. It is a very interesting book to read, as it focuses on some good <u>facts on the Bible</u>.

BIBLE FUN FACTS

Old and New Testament Facts . . .

- Did you know the word Bible comes from the Greek word Biblia, meaning; books. No wonder it's called the Bible: it's a collection of 66 wonderful books!

- Did you know the Bible contains 773, 693 words and 3,566,480 letters. Reading them all aloud would take a person approximately 70 hours!

- The Old Testament has 39 books, while the New Testament has 27 books, bringing the total to 66. Of the 27 books of the New Testament, the Apostle Paul wrote 14 books (more than half) of the New Testament.

- The Bible contains 1189 chapters.

- The word 'testament' means 'contract' or 'covenant'.

- The Old Testament was written in Hebrew.

- The New Testament was written in Greek.

First and the Last . . .

- The first three words in the Bible are 'in the beginning'.

- The first five books of the Bible, referred to as the Pentateuch were written by Moses.

- The last word in the Bible is 'Amen'.

Longest and the Shortest . . .

- The shortest book in the Bible is John 3 with one chapter, 13 verses.

- The shortest verse in the Bible is John 11: 35, 'Jesus wept'.

- The longest book in the Bible is Psalm.

- The longest verse is Esther 8:9 containing 90 words.

- The longest word in the Bible is Mahershalalhashbaz (Isaiah 8:1). It's going to be a problem for those with fear of long words!

Strongest, Wisest, Oldest, Tallest . . .

- The strongest and wisest men in the Bible are the two sons: Samson and Solomon.

- The tallest and biggest villain in the Bible is Goliath whose height was over 9 ½ feet.

- The greatest warrior in the Bible is Gideon, who defeated 135, 000 Midianites along with 300 men and 300 trumpets under God's power.

- The oldest individual in the Bible was Methuselah (Genesis 5:27), who died at the age of 969!

- The oldest parable in the Bible is in Judges 9:8-15.

Did you know . . .

- Psalm 117, 118 and 119 are chapters with special significance in the Bible. Apparently, Psalm 117 is the shortest chapter in the Bible, Psalm 118 is the central chapter of the Bible and Psalm 119 is the longest chapter in the Bible. It's a hat trick for the Psalm!

- Ezra 7:21 contains all the letters of the alphabet, except 'J'.

- The word 'God' appears 3,358 times in the Bible.

- Did you know the first baptism in the Bible was conducted by Moses, who used ox's blood to baptize the people?

- The sheep is the most frequently mentioned animal in the Bible.

- Did you know the only domesticated animal not mentioned in the Bible is the cat?

- The phrase 'do not be afraid' appears 365 times in the Bible, just as the number of days in a year. This phrase is not a suggestion but a command. So as we live each day, we know God has commanded us to trust Him with all our heart and be at rest!

BIBLE FACTS

Comprising of 39 books, without counting the Apocrypha, the Old Testaments was written in Hebrew originally.

The books that make up the Old Testament are: Genesis; Exodus; Leviticus Numbers; Deuteronomy; Joshua; Judges; Ruth; 1 & 2 Samuel; 1 & 2 Kings; 1 & 2 Chronicles; Ezra; Nehemiah; Esther; Job; Psalm; Proverbs; Ecclesiastes; Song of Songs; Isaiah; Jeremiah; Lamentations; Ezekiel; Daniel; Hosea; Joel; Amos; Obadiah; Jonah; Micah; Nahum; Habakkuk; Zephaniah; Haggai; Zechariah; and Malachi.

Amongst these, the first five are referred to as the Torah, or the Pentateuch, or the Five Books of Moses. Traditionally, they are thought to have been authored by Moses, although modern scholars think that they may have been written by 4-5 authors. The only book amongst these where the word 'God' is not mentioned is the book of Esther.

Apart from the Hebrew Scripture, the Bible that most Christians use comprises of the life and teachings of Jesus Christ, along with the Apostle Paul's letters and also the writings of other disciples, as well as the early church along with the Book of Revelation.

Written originally in Greek, although some people argue that it was written in Aramaic first, the New Testament comprises of 27 books, which are: Matthew; Mark; Luke; John; Acts; Romans; 1 & 2 Corinthians; Galatians; Ephesians; Philippians; Colossians; 1 & 2

Thessalonians; 1 & 2 Timothy; Titus; Philemon; Hebrews; James; 1 & 2 Peter; 1, 2 & 3 John; Jude; and Revelation.

It is said that about 40 people wrote the Bible, starting from about 1450 B.C. to about 100 A.D.

The Bible is made up of several genres of literature such as myth, poetry, prophecy, narrative, letters, and sermonic literature.

The Bible was first translated into English by John Wycliffe, in 1382 A.D.

The first book that was printed was the Bible, in 1454 A.D. This was accomplished by Johannes Gutenberg, the inventor of the 'type mold' used in the printing press.

The Bible, since then, has been translated into more than 2000 languages, and continues to be the largest seller amongst published books.

THE BIBLE TELLS ME SO

Jesus loves me! this I know,
For the Bible tells me so.
Little ones to Him belong;
they are weak but He is strong.

Yes, Jesus loves me!
Yes, Jesus loves me!
Yes, Jesus loves me!
The Bible tells me so.

THIS LITTLE LIGHT OF MINE

This little light of mine, I'm gonna let it shine.
This little light of mine, I'm gonna let it shine,
let it shine, let it shine, let it shine.

Let it shine til Jesus comes.
I'm gonna let it shine.
Let it shine til Jesus comes.
I'm gonna let it shine, let it shine, let it shine,
let it shine.

Let it shine over the whole wide world,
I'm gonna let it shine.
Let it shine over the whole wide world,
I'm gonna let it shine, let it shine, let it shine,
let it shine.

FAMOUS PEOPLE ON THE BIBLE

Ulysses S. Grant

"To the influence of this book we are indebted for the progress made in civilization, and to this we must look as our guide in the future."

Abraham Lincoln

"This great book . . . is the best gift God has given to man."

Woodrow Wilson

"A man has found himself when he has found his relation to the rest of the universe, and here is the Book in which those relations are set forth."

John Quincy Adams

"Great is my veneration for the Bible."

Sir Isaac Newton

"There are more sure marks of authenticity in the Bible than in any profane history."

Charles Dickens

"The New Testament is the best book the world has ever known or will know.

Queen Victoria

"England has become great and happy by the knowledge of the true God through Jesus Christ . . . . This is the secret of England's greatness.

Mark Twain

"It is hard to make a choice of the most beautiful passage in a Book which is gemmed with beautiful passages as the Bible.

Robert E. Lee

"In all my perplexities and distresses, the Bible has never failed to give me light and strength.

Thomas Jefferson

"The studious perusal of the sacred volume will make better citizens, better fathers, and better husbands."

Galileo

"I believe that the intention of Holy Writ was to persuade men of the truths necessary to salvation."

Tim Tebow

John 3:16

In 2009 the Florida Gators played the Oklahoma Sooners at the Orange Bowl for the national championship. Florida's quarterback, Tim Tebow, lead the Gators to a 24-14 victory, capturing the 2008 national title. Like many college and professional football players, Tim Tebow wears eye black to reduce the light glare that can impede seeing an airborne football. Unlike most players, Tim boldly professes his faith in Jesus Christ by applying scripture to his eye black. Tebow, the 2007 Heisman Trophy Winner, often sports Philippians 4:13, which reads, "I can do all things through Christ who strengthens me." On January 8, 2009, at the Orange Bowl before a national audience, the message on Tim Tebow's eyeblack was John 3:16. The following morning, Google reported that John 3:16 was the #1 ranked Hot Trends search.

MORE FAVORITE VERSES

The LORD is my rock, my fortress and my deliverer; my God is my
rock, in whom I take refuge. He is my shield and the horn of my
salvation, my stronghold.

Psalm 18:2

Your word is a lamp to my feet and a light for my path.

Psalm 119:105

Beloved, if God has so loved us, we also ought to love one another.

1 John 4:11

For nothing will be impossible with God.

Luke 1:37

Fear not, Jacob, my servant," says the LORD, "for I am with you.
I will destroy the nations to which I have exiled you, but I will
not destroy you. But I must discipline you; I cannot let you go
unpunished."

Jeremiah 46:28

Be ye kind one to another, tenderhearted, forgiving one another, even
as God for Christ's sake hath forgiven you.
Ephesians 4:32

Teaching them to observe all things whatsoever I have commanded
you: and, lo, I am with you always, [even] unto the end of the world.
Amen.
Matthew 20: 12

I can do all things through Christ who strengthens me.
Philippians 4:13

But those who hope in the LORD will renew their strength.
They will soar on wings like eagles; they will run and not grow weary,
they will walk and not be faint.
Isaiah 40:31

But seek first his kingdom and his righteousness, and all these things
will be given to you as well.
Matthew 6:33

Do not let this Book of the Law depart from your mouth; meditate
on it day and night, so that you may be careful to do everything
written in it. Then you will be prosperous and successful.
Joshua 1:8

Trust in the LORD with all your heart and lean not on your own
understanding; in all your ways acknowledge him, and

he will make your paths straight.
Proverbs 3:5-6

Delight yourself in the LORD and he will give you
the desires of your heart.
Psalm 37:4

This is the day the LORD has made; let us rejoice and be glad in it.
Psalm 118:24

May my prayer be set before you like incense; may the lifting up of
my hands be like the evening sacrifice.
Psalm 141:2

Yours, O LORD, is the greatness and the power and the glory and the
majesty and the splendor, for everything in heaven and earth is yours.
Yours, O LORD, is the kingdom; you are exalted as head over all.
1 Chronicles 29:11

"If we confess our sins, he is faithful and just and will forgive us our
sins and purify us from all unrighteousness."
1 John 1:9

Always giving thanks to God the Father for everything, in the name
of our Lord Jesus Christ.
Ephesians 5:20

Ask and it will be given to you; seek and you will find; knock and the
door will be opened to you. Matthew 7:7

Psalm 23

The LORD is my shepherd; I shall not want.

He maketh me to lie down in green pastures: he leadeth me beside
the still waters.

He restoreth my soul: he leadeth me in the paths of righteousness for
his name's sake.

Yea, though I walk through the valley of the shadow of death, I will fear
no evil: for thou art with me; thy rod and thy staff they comfort me.

Thou preparest a table before me in the presence of mine enemies:
thou anointest my head with oil; my cup runneth over.

Surely goodness and mercy shall follow me all the days of my life: and
I will dwell in the house of the LORD forever.

Psalm 100

"Make a joyful noise to the Lord, all the Earth

Worship the Lord with gladness; come into his presence with singing.
Know that the Lord is God.

It is he, who made us, and we are his; we are his people and the sheep
of his pasture.

Enter his gates with thanksgiving, and his courts with praise.
Give thanks to him, bless his name.

For the Lord is good; his steadfast love endureth forever, and his
faithfulness to all generations."

BEATITUDES

The Beatitudes from the Sermon on the Mount
When Jesus saw the crowds, he went up the mountain; and after he
sat down, his disciples came to him.
Then he began to speak, and taught them, saying:
Blessed are the poor in spirit, for theirs is the kingdom of heaven.
Blessed are those who mourn, for they will be comforted.
Blessed are the meek, for they will inherit the earth.
Blessed are those who hunger and thirst for righteousness, for they
will be filled.
Blessed are the merciful, for they will receive mercy.
Blessed are the pure in heart, for they will see God.
Blessed are the peacemakers, for they will be called children of God.
Blessed are those who are persecuted for righteousness' sake, for theirs
is the kingdom of heaven.
Blessed are you when people revile you and persecute you and utter
all kinds of evil against you falsely on my account.
Rejoice and be glad, for your reward is great in heaven, for in the
same way they persecuted the prophets before you.

Matthew Chapter 5
New Testament

MATTHEW 5: 1-12

1 Corinthians 13:4-13

Love is patient, love is kind. It does not envy, it does not boast, it is not proud. It is not rude, it is not self-seeking, it is not easily angered, and it keeps no record of wrongs. Love does not delight in evil but rejoices with the truth. It always protects, always trusts, always hopes, and always perseveres. Love never fails. But where there are prophecies, they will cease; where there are tongues, they will be stilled; where there is knowledge, it will pass away. For we know in part and we prophesy in part, but when perfection comes, the imperfect disappears. When I was a child, I talked like a child; I thought like a child, I reasoned like a child. When I became a man, I put childish ways behind me. Now we see but a poor reflection as in a mirror; then we shall see face to face. Now I know in part; then I shall know fully, even as I am fully known. And now these three remain: faith, hope and love. But the greatest of these is love.

TEN COMMANDMENTS

Exodus 20:3-17

You shall have no other gods before me.

You shall not make for yourself an idol in the form of anything in heaven above or on the earth beneath or in the waters below.

You shall not bow down to them or worship them; for I, the LORD your God, am a jealous God, punishing the children for the sin of the fathers to the third and fourth generation of those who hate me, but showing love to a thousand {generations} of those who love me and keep my commandments.

You shall not misuse the name of the LORD your God, for the LORD will not hold anyone guiltless who misuses his name.

Remember the Sabbath day by keeping it holy.

Honor your father and your mother.

You shall not murder.

You shall not commit adultery.

You shall not steal.

You shall not give false testimony against your neighbor.

You shall not covet your neighbor or anything that belongs to your neighbor.